Living OUT LOUD

Activities to fuel a creative Life.

by Keri Smith

CHRONICLE BOOKS

SAN FRANCISCO

Design by Laura Crookston
Manufactured in China

ISBN 978-0-8118-3674-6

10 9 8 7 6 5 4

Chronicle Books, LLC
680 Second Street
San Francisco, CA 94107
www.chroniclebooks.com

Excerpts from *Hundreds and Thousands: The Journals of an Artist* by Emily Carr, © 1966. Reprinted with the permission of Stoddart Publishing Co. Ltd.

Excerpts from *The Diary of Anaïs Nin–Volume 3* by Anaïs Nin, © 1969. Reprinted with the permission of Harcourt Brace.

Excerpts from *Writing Down the Bones* by Natalie Goldberg, © 1986 by Natalie Goldberg. Reprinted by arrangement with Shambhala Publications, Inc., Boston, www.shambhala.com

Excerpts from *If You Want to Write* by Brenda Ueland, © 1987 by the Estate of Brenda Ueland. Reprinted with the permission of Graywolf Press, Saint Paul, Minnesota.

Contents

Starting

Connecting

Letting Go

Dreaming Work

Starting

Introduction

Several years ago I started writing a column called "The Wish Jar Tales—Living on Purpose Every Day" for a local arts paper. The column explored creativity, inspiration, fear, courage, and learning by doing. My writing attracted a following of people from all walks of life who shared a common goal: to find the courage to make a living doing what they love (or at least to do more of what they love on a daily basis).

One of the features I wrote, "How to Make a Living Doing What You Love," received an overwhelming response. I encouraged readers to photocopy the column and pass it on to their friends. In this way, "The Wish Jar Tales" became a way for us to come together and to build a creative community.

CREATIVE INSPIRATION IS CONTAGIOUS!!!

I have read dozens of books on creativity, and followed many programs, regimens, and exercises, only to feel my energy dwindle and my motivation fade. Let's face it, most creative beings are NOT regimented. (They're not even people who can eat meals at the same time every day!)

My favorite books are those that make me burst with energy and inspire me to drop everything and get down onto the floor and fearlessly create for hours. *Living Out Loud* is a "to do" book, not a "how to" book. I hope it will encourage you to play, and to face the fears that hold you back.

Here is my realization:
Play is the most important element in discovering who you are. Play will lead you right into your deepest desires.

As creative individuals, we share the tendency to become easily overwhelmed by taking on too much at one time, especially when starting a new career or creative endeavor. We need to learn to slow down and enjoy the process. Then we are much more likely to follow our dreams and, as a result, attract like-minded people who share our vision.

Be present. Enjoy yourself. Trust that your body remembers what it feels like to play. Move from your center. Gain strength from one another, and walk forward together with courage. The universe is waiting . . .

You will find playful exercises to try throughout the book. Most of them take less than an hour, and some only 10 minutes! They will help you rediscover your creative center, and you'll realize that it's been there all along!

Starting

FINDING TRUE PASSION

*The aim of life is to live, and to live means to be
aware, joyously, drunkenly, serenely, divinely aware.*
—Henry Miller

Children possess this divine awareness. They are
naturally joyous and passionate. They also instinctively
know what they want, and they find ways to act on
their instincts, doing exactly what they want.

Childhood memories carry us back to a time of inspiration, excitement, and joy. Re-creating childhood
stories and myths allows us to remember a time
when passion was foremost and to reconnect with
our true selves—the part of ourselves that is not
defined by family or financial and social obligations.

While we may be ready to do what we love, we're
not always sure what that may be. How do you start?
Think back to your earliest experiences of play. What
did play mean to you? Digging in the dirt? Making
things out of wood? Exploring nature? Caring for
animals? Writing plays? What activities allowed
you to lose all sense of time and space?

As children, my sister and I used to build dream houses filled with tiny imaginative rooms, secret passageways, furniture, mazes, and even characters. Today I still have a passion for creating little worlds and characters to interact within my art.

Once you have determined what you loved doing as a child, it helps to figure out what, exactly, excited you about that activity. Reading, for example, is a favorite childhood pastime. The books you chose as a child will give many clues about the things that move you. Were the characters involved in adventures? Solving mysteries? Were they funny? Smart? If you had a favorite book, what did you particularly like about it?

If you spent hours riding your bike, were you excited about racing? Competing with others? Feeling the sense of freedom? When you figure out what moved you, you can start to work it into a possible career concept. Here are some clues:

If your childhood passion was reading, there are several avenues you could pursue. If you loved the feeling of being among books in a library or bookstore setting, you might look into the field of publishing or bookselling. If you were in awe of those who could create such wonderful stories, writing might be an avenue to try. Maybe you loved creating dozens of outfits for your dolls; this might indicate that fashion design is something for you to consider. Get to the root of your passion.

During the bulk of your activity, did you play alone or with others? While most children like to play in a group setting, others get equal enjoyment playing by themselves. Your recollections will tell you if you are better suited to a group setting or a career in which you work alone.

Starting to play again can induce fear. Somewhere along the way you may have learned that play was frivolous and a waste of precious "work" (i.e., money-making) time. It is a common belief in our culture that it is not possible to work and play at the same time. Your inner critic will probably remind you of this many times along the way. But finding and pursuing your passion will in the long run lead to a life that fulfills you in all ways. In the beginning you will be going against what our culture wants to do. When you go outside the norm and take your own path, it is quite normal to have doubts about what you are doing. Find all the wonderful people in the world who will support you as you push past the fear to reclaim your playful self and find a new way of being. (On the way, smile at your inner critic and say, "I'm not listening to you anymore!!!")

Connect with others who have been where you want to go. Join organizations, do searches on the Internet for like-minded souls, write letters to famous people in your field, attend a conference, start your own group (you could even create on on-line newsgroup). Teach the things you most need to learn (begin by inspiring others to investigate your field—this is one of the best ways to establish yourself in a given area). Do an apprenticeship with an expert, or volunteer your time with related not-for-profit organizations. For example, writer Alex Beauchamp wanted to connect with other successful women, so she created www.anothergirlatplay.com, a Web site that documents the creative process and inspires others to do the same.

Read about what it was like to begin something new, especially in the moments of darkness, futility, anxiety, and doubt. Learn about the experiences of successful people. They will help keep your feelings in perspective, and they'll serve as role models. You have permission to exclaim, "I can do it, too!"

Bring your childhood sense of play to your everyday life. This is your gift. It is unique to you. It is the key to *living out loud* in the present moment.

ACTIVITY

Momentous Play

IT DOESN'T GET MUCH BETTER THAN THIS!

Get down on the floor and play this week. Lose yourself in the present moment and conjure up happy creative energy. Don't focus on the finished product. **PLAY** is what it's all about! Why do we forget?

Suggestions

1. Doodle wildly (try new colors or techniques).

2. Make a paper doll of yourself (have fun with the accessories).

3. Make origami lanterns in all colors and hang them in your work space.

4. Knit or crochet something fun and meaningful (perhaps a little journal cover).

5. Reread your favorite children's books (lose yourself).

6. Dress up just for fun (experiment with wild colors).

7. Sew a rag doll (based on yourself as a child).

8. Make cookies in spectacular shapes (create your dream home out of gingerbread).

9. Self-publish a magic book (see page 61).

How to Wreck a Sketchbook

CONFRONTING THE INNER CRITIC WITH GUSTO

Buy a new sketchbook. Start to write. Let the words fill the pages. In a matter of hours the stark white sheets will be overcome with thick and thin lines. Let words and letters of all sizes appear carelessly and comfortably without fear.

You are invited to let the idea be more important than the execution. Let your thoughts flow onto the page. First thoughts are usually the most spontaneous, intuitive, and daring. Let the book fill up with your first thoughts. Silence the second thoughts. Put the second thoughts in a soundproof container. (A mason jar with a tightly fitting lid works well for this.) Let them ramble on, but do not pay any attention.

A sketchbook does not have to be a sacred place where ideas cannot exist without the promise of greatness. Greatness often appears in the midst of imperfection and makes regular visits to the "Land of Mistakes." The Land of Mistakes is the place we learned to avoid when we got to a certain age. We were judged by how well we could color within the lines. Entering the Land of Mistakes means coloring outside the lines on purpose. It is a place where anything is allowed, risks are taken, and we are encouraged to try new things. We might get dirty in the process; that is good. Some of your best work can come from

15

playful experimenting. Maybe you should exile your-self to the Land of Mistakes so that you can become friends with the fear of being wrong. Mess things up on PURPOSE! Write or draw anything that comes into your head. Scribble frantically. Let the blank page know that you want to be wrong!

Scream "I DON'T CARE!" from the tip of your pen. Let the mistakes seep into the cracks and fibers of the book. Let little pools of ink run dangerously into, and through, other pages, threatening to alter what's already been written. Carelessly tear the pages. Listen to the marvelous and unnerving sound of fibers ripping. Ooh, that's good. Smear chocolate. Coffee anyone?

If your spontaneity dwindles, set free your destructive side. Write the word "precious" on a page. Deface it. That feels good, doesn't it? If necessary, do the same to the words "can't," "should," and "sorry." When the inner critic shows up (and it will), sit it down, make tea, and ask, "Does this make you uncomfortable?" Make a detailed list of all the things your inner critic is saying. Carefully tear that page out of the book. Rip it into very small pieces and dramatically launch it into the closest body of water (preferably a toilet). With as much enthusiasm as you can muster, proclaim, **"YOU ARE NOT THE BOSS OF ME!!!"** *Flush.*

Continue this process until the book is full or until you collapse, exhausted and triumphant, onto the couch, whichever comes first.

afraid of the blank page

The following is an inner dialogue I had one day while having self-doubts. The blue parts are the questions and the pink are the answers. We always know the answers we are seeking.

Am I an artist? How do I begin? I'm afraid to start. Pretend it's your journal. Just scribble. Every mark is valid.

JUMP! Don't make a BIG production out of it.

Draw on the floor. Start with a line. Let it happen. But I want it to be good. Good & bad don't exist here. Begin. But it's painful... It's more painful not to. What if I hate it? It's not YOURS to judge. How do you know all this ??? We've been here before. I'm afraid to let go, show myself as I really am. You are O.K. I secretly don't think I'm a good artist... there's that word again.

⤳ Judgment is a choice we make.

Just be honest in your intentions. HONEST with yourself. Play more. Think less. Does everybody feel this way? Yes, EVERYBODY. Keep doing your own thing...

ACTIVITY

Originality is a topic many creative souls constantly struggle with. The quest for originality comes from a desire to be seen and heard, and to make a mark in a world that seems resistant to change.

As creative beings, we have the gift of taking all of our experiences, embracing them, and using them as a source for our work. The things in your life that you have struggled to overcome and deal with enable you to see the world differently from others. Your multitude of experiences and perceptions has never been reproduced by any other human being. Because of this, your knowledge and vision are different from everyone else's. Use this to your advantage. History is full of exceptional people who have allowed their own visions to propel them.

Each person speaks from his or her accumulation of experiences. How, then, could your own experience not be unique? How have negative experiences changed your perceptions? How can you apply your life experience to new uses?

Look at your life as a source for new creative ideas. How did where you grew up shape your view of things?

One method of creating original ideas is to combine two or more ideas that have not been merged before, like combining bookbinding with the computer, suburban architecture with knitting, seashells with papermaking, subway riding with painting.

Escape from conventional methods and ideas.

Here's a simple exercise from an old teacher of mine: Write down as many uses as you can think of for a pencil.

Try to get to 100.

creating a SACRED space
...right in your own home!

The Comfort Zone
A cozy chair, your favorite books & a pot of tea.

The Altar
Set up icons, candles, incense, and pictures of things that move you... say a prayer.

We all need our own little piece of the world to retreat to. It can be used to escape, to recharge, to divulge, to create a ritual, or to just 'be'. Choose one that most invokes your sense of adventure. Curl up... breathe.

The Arabian Nights
Set up a tent or make a blanket fort. Fill it with pillows, snacks, and your journal. Don't forget the exotic music.

The Personal Spa
Fill your bathroom with candles, essential oils, and mud masks. Sink into a bubble-filled tub. Unravel.

Unlimited Life Plan

DETERMINING A DESTINATION

At the center of your being you have the answer, you know who you are and you know what you want.
—Lao Tzu

We are here at this point because we have questions. How do we create the life and career that we want? Where do we start? What direction do we take? In order to manifest new energy and success in our lives we need to create a detailed image of what the next destination looks like and formalize a map for getting there.

This is the most helpful exercise we can do to put ourselves on the road to achieving our greatest individual potential. Only by asking can we bring into being a self-directed, empowered, and meaningful life.

In the past I've always had great difficulty defining my next destination, out of lack of discipline and fear of not finishing, but I've found this exercise is the most effective in giving focus to my life and career. I have learned to set my intention and define my wants. I still ask questions, but now I rely on my vision and my map to bring me back on course. After a period of weeks, months, or even years, I am amazed to find myself at my destination. Getting there was accomplished by taking very small steps over a long period of time.

You can do it, too! Begin by creating a detailed image of your ideal life. Put it on paper; make it as full and as decadent as you wish. Dream big. This is your chance to conjure up all your innermost desires. Inside each of us is a picture of a destination where we would experience the greatest fulfillment. Sometimes it helps to use a model, someone whose life you admire or wish to emulate. Maybe it's a favorite author who lives in a house by the sea, or a travel writer who travels to exotic places. Let that picture be a starting point for your own passionate journey. Age is not a factor here. You can reinvent your life at any time.

Answer the following questions as if you were already living your ideal life. Get into character! Think big! It's your ideal life—you can pretend anything! (Or just start writing stream of consciousness!)

1. Where do you live? Describe what your home looks like.
2. What kind of people have you surrounded yourself with?
3. Who are your best friends? What makes those relationships work?
4. What do you do on a daily basis that fulfills your emotional, spiritual, and physical needs?

5. Look at the clothes you are wearing. What do they say about you?
6. How would you describe your chosen profession?
7. Describe your work setting.
8. Whom do you work with?
9. Describe your ideal client and your ideal working relationship.
10. What do you enjoy most about your career?
11. How much money do you make?
12. What do you spend your money on?
13. Have you acquired any awards and honors?
14. Describe how you think your peers view you.
15. How do you view yourself?
16. What do your admirers say about you and your work?
17. What would you like to contribute to your field?
18. What would you like to contribute to your community?
19. How do you enjoy your spare time?

Your Life is Your Art

AN INVESTIGATION INTO SOURCES

One summer morning, I came upon a girl selling wildflower bouquets in glass jars at the local farmers' market. The beauty of these small treasures, so lovingly assembled with a careful eye, transfixed me. I thought, "This is ART!" She had captured, in a somewhat naïve way, something that arises out of everyday life. This is the nature of "honest art."

In their teachings, the renowned designers Charles and Ray Eames discuss the importance of source. You cannot create art without a source, although the nature of what makes a good source is sometimes elusive to the maker. The things you do naturally every day are your greatest sources. Look at your daily life, paying attention to what you do without thinking. Look at the things around you. The sites in your neighborhood as you take a walk. A phone conversation. A new purse. Your favorite cup. A hole in your shoe. The contents of your knapsack. Your lunch. Include the ugly parts, which we often discard. The mess on your desk. A painful childhood memory. A nagging fear. A terrible fight. A death.

Use all these as sources in your opus. Write them down. Paint them out. Transform them. Change their meaning. It is all worthy of documenting. Your view of the world is unique and people will respond to your work when it is honest.

You might not see beauty, but sometimes that is better. Just get it out. Talk about what you did yesterday. My favorite saying is "Use what you've got!" Just start!

Close your eyes. Slowly open them and write about the first thing you see. Try to imagine that you are seeing it for the first time. Look first at the bottom half of the object or person or view. Have a conversation with that part. Now try the top half.

ACTIVITY

Recipe Box of Secrets

BE YOUR OWN RESEARCH PROJECT

We are all collectors at heart. Creating a Box of Secrets gives you the chance to explore and to research things that will help you see the big picture when you need perspective.

Directions

1. Find a good-size box (a large shoebox works well), and get a stack of card stock or index cards to fit the box. The benefit of using a box is that it allows you to move things around, enabling you to make new connections between things you are drawn to.
2. Collect recipes, inspiring newspaper clippings, colors, textures, and quotes—whatever moves you!
3. Notice when items begin to relate to one another. Make categories for them and let the categories evolve and change. You will start to see how everything is related at a root level. (I found myself collecting articles about artists' houses. At first I thought it was the artists' work that moved me, but I discovered that I am actually in love with the process of making art, and the lifestyle that goes with it.)
4. Use the Box of Secrets as inspiration for *living out loud.*

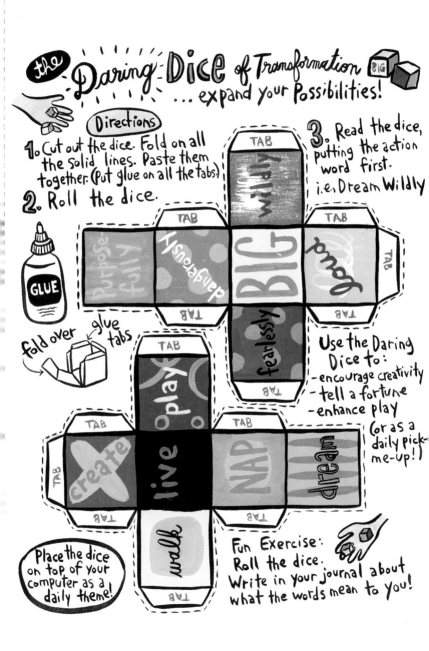

Closer to Fine

FACING THE FEARS

The week I turned thirty I made a list of "Thirty Things to Do in My Thirtieth Year." I wanted to move forward into a new decade with power and excitement. Many things on the list were relatively small and easy to accomplish: Enjoy a long walk on the beach, eat a fresh lobster, plant a rosebush for my mom. Some of the things were more intimidating: Write a book, learn to drive. These thirty things were a way of pushing myself out beyond my known world.

One of the difficult things for me to do was singing in public. When I mentioned this to one of my friends, an accomplished folksinger, her eyes lit up, and she invited me to do a song with her group at its next show. My reaction was one of giddy excitement, which quickly gave way to fear. (Singing around a bonfire is more what I'd had in mind.) "But isn't this what you wanted?" I asked myself. "What's better than an opportunity with a deadline?" I had to try.

The show was more than a month away, providing ample time to rehearse and work on my voice. But could I sing? I had not sung since sixth-grade choir, when my best friend let me know it might be better to spend my time on other things. Even though I loved to sing, I had never sung again.

I was pleasantly surprised by my first rehearsal with the group. We managed to learn the song and get some harmonies down relatively quickly. To my untrained ear it sounded on key and actually quite good, but could I really pull this off? We had chosen "Closer to Fine," by the Indigo Girls, a tune that talks about moving beyond comfort zones and taking life less seriously, something I had hoped this whole experience would help me with.

After weeks of practice and lots of support, I had an epiphany: I cared too much about what other people thought. I worried that if I sang poorly, people might think less of me. I had to be willing to fail! I had to surrender to the process and let it happen. I finally realized that I made my list to push MYSELF, not to impress OTHERS.

On the night of the performance, the cafe was packed. There was an electric buzz and energy in the place. Although I wasn't singing until halfway through the second set, I started to lose feeling in my arms. I said a silent prayer to whoever would listen. When it was my turn, I seemed to float in the direction of the stage. I pulled up a stool for support. The audience which had been so rowdy, now sat silent and transfixed, with all eyes on me. And in that moment all my fear vanished.

I told the audience about my list of thirty things, and people cheered. Then I knew that everyone in the room was with me. I had no fear because they had joined me on my journey, and I could not fail because I had already succeeded in pushing myself. As we held the last note, the place erupted into wild applause. I screamed into the microphone, "I did it!" More applause. I was on top of the world. People ran to hug me as I left the stage. A woman with tears in her eyes said, "Thank you. You've given me courage to face my own fears."

I have learned that we must never underestimate the power that facing our fears has on other people. We help the world to be stronger when we ourselves become stronger.

ACTIVITY

Challenge Yourself

Create a list of the things you've always wanted to do but never found the time or courage to try. Choose your top five and take baby steps to becoming *closer to fine.*

_____

_____

_____

_____

_____

_____

_____

_____

_____

_____

_____

_____

_____

_____

the Magnificent World of Sense shopping

An ode to the ordinary. No need to spend a lot of cash just be present...

Wander aimlessly, Write down what you find.

orange blossom tea
freesias
wood-burning stove
soap
smell
books
sheets dried on the clothesline
cumin
samosas

fuzzy green sweater
ladybug
rain
shiny eggplant
ice
touch
fur
brown paper packages
flannel

black licorice
garlic
snow
café latté
lemon
taste
POPSICLE
lipstick
soba noodles
anise

church bells
a child laughing
small dog
BIRDS
LISTEN
high heels
conversation
music

ACTIVITY

ONE OF MY FAVORITE THINGS TO DO

Charles and Ray Eames praised the use of a finder in their teachings. A finder is a small piece of cardboard (about three-by-four inches) with a one-inch-square hole cut out of the middle. Viewing the world through this hole forces you to lose context and content, and to greatly shift your perception. The finder allows you to focus on small sections and negative space. It also singles out color and isolates pattern.

Make a finder* and place it on a stack of magazines. Cut through as many layers as you can with an X-Acto knife. Sort through the pieces, picking out the ones you like. Look at the shapes you've created by accident. Use the cut-out squares as reference for other projects or to create new ideas, concepts, and compositions.

Take the finder with you on a walk. Look at familiar places with a new eye. In your sketchbook, sketch out what you see. What do you notice that you didn't see before?

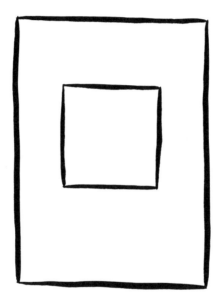

* Photocopy this page- that way you can
make unlimited finders for yourself!

Transformative PLAY

FOR SHORT ATTENTION SPANS

Fun things to do in under an hour

Neck Purse of small secrets

Knit a long rectangle. Sew up the sides to create a "pocket". Leave a flap. Create a long chain for the strap. Add button. Insert "secrets".

sew here

PAPIER Maché Beads

1. Make a paste out of flour & water.
2. Dip long strips of paper in paste.
3. Wrap around nails.
4. Let dry, then paint.

Decorate with Origami

Make as many cranes as you can out of colorful squares of paper. String them together for a cool mobile.

Word Tree

Take paper or cardboard and using bright colors paint a dozen inspiring words to describe yourself. Cut them out and hang with string.

GLASS lanterns

Find some old glass jars. Start collaging the outside with thin bits of paper & glue stick. Fill the bottom with sand & add a candle. (You can also use flowers & leaves, or whatever you like.)

Connecting

GETTING THROUGH THE HARD TIMES

When my mother was dying of cancer, my journal became my outlet. My journal was someone I could tell anything to when it was hard talking to family and to others. It was my comfort. One day at the hospital, I reached a point where I couldn't take it anymore. I was emotionally and physically drained. Even the tears had stopped. My body mirrored my heaviness: head down, shallow breath, empty eyes.

I wandered into a lounge designated for family members and stared at the small garden outside the window. As I turned, a dog-eared book sitting on the bookshelf caught my eye. It was Anne Frank's *Diary of a Young Girl.* I opened it up to these words:

The best remedy for those who are afraid, lonely, or unhappy is to go outside, somewhere where they can be quiet, alone with the heavens, nature and God. Because only then does one feel that all is as it should be and that God wishes to see people happy, amidst the simple beauty of nature. As long as this exists, and it certainly always will, I know that then there will always be comfort for every sorrow, whatever the circumstances may be. And I firmly believe that nature brings solace in all troubles.

In that moment I knew I could continue. The serendipitous reading of the words of a 14-year-old girl who lived in another time and another world inspired me. She lived in daily fear, but she communicated unimaginable strength and faith through her writing.

When I left the hospital that night, I felt the wind on my face for the first time in weeks. I noticed a lone tree and stared at it. I got on a bus and looked out the window, transfixed by what I saw. The odd flower. Trees by the roadside. The wide open sky. I felt like yelling, "Anne, I understand!! I see it!! You are here too!!" I smiled with tears trickling down my face.

When I read Anne's words I knew that I was not alone, that this was not personal, and that the pain I was experiencing was universal. The message was that we are all connected through our experiences of grief and loss. In reading other people's diaries and journals we see that the way through suffering is to just be present, aware, and find comfort in the simple things. By reading someone else's words we feel connected to others, and by writing our own words we connect with ourselves.

Anne Frank wrote to feel better, but her words helped me to feel better, too. This is the power of words, especially those that come from experiences of intense pain. And this is why your journal can be a friend.

Women Writers

In the depths of cold and austere winter, I find myself needing to retreat to the comfort that only inspiring books can provide. To me, it's not unlike the warmth of a bowl of homemade soup.

I am drawn to biographies and journals that speak of survival, triumph over adversity, and the need to create even in the face of suffering. I have been led to the most wonderful collection of women writers who continued to endeavor through moments of hopelessness and extended periods of self-doubt.

Here is a quick list:
May Sarton, Natalie Goldberg, Colette, Sue Bender, Anaïs Nin, Anne Frank, Anne Morrow Lindbergh, Opal Whiteley, and Maya Angelou.

How did these women find the constant courage and confidence to believe in themselves? These are some of the characteristics I've noticed that they all share:
1. A passion for nature.
2. A connection with something greater than themselves.
3. A connection with childhood memories.
4. A connection to other artists, writers, and creators.

5. A sharing of ideas and inspiration: creative gatherings, dinners, support groups, cafe meetings, letter writing, afternoon teas.
6. A need for, and a confidence in, solitude.
7. A capacity for self-motivation: inspiring walks, travel, learning new skills, reading, cooking, exploring.
8. An experience of pain, and the triumph of moving beyond it to create a well of strength.
9. A gift of mindfulness and an ability to see magic in the ordinary.
10. An experience of gratefulness and compassion for all the good things and people in their lives.

These are the qualities we must nurture and encourage in ourselves. Give yourself permission to temporarily retreat and to receive nourishment from those who have gone before and from those who have had the courage to write it down.

ACTIVITY

Connections

MAGIC ORACLES

In British filmmaker Mike Leigh's *Career Girls,* two friends play a game in which they each ask a question about the future. Chanting to the spirit of Emily Brontë, they open *Wuthering Heights* and read from random passages. Thus the oracle speaks and gives them the answer.

Choose a book, or two. Maybe it's an old favorite, or a library book, or even the phone book. Close your eyes, ask the question, and open the book to see what you find. Let the oracle tell you the thing you most need to hear.

Ten Things I've Learned From Women

A large circle of creative women has always surrounded me. It's helped form the person I am today. This circle started during my mother's early teens, as she forged bonds with friends that carried her through adolescence and the milestones of marriage, childbirth, and death. Now in their fifties, these women are more aware of their power and demonstrate it by partaking in creative rituals and gatherings. It is during these gatherings that they solidify their sense of connection with themselves and one another.

When my mother died of cancer, there was a painful void left in this circle of friends. But the women responded with their usual strength and unrelenting will. They moved swiftly to surround my sister and me with maternal love and guidance. In our grieving, we were able to trust and surrender to the familiarity they provided us.

It is exciting to see that the second-generation circle of creative women has inherited this sense of power and love. We understand the lessons taught to us by our mothers. We know how lucky we are to have these intensely creative women in our lives and to see ourselves through them.

I've been working on a list of things that I have learned from two generations of creative women. It is not complete. I will be unwrapping the gifts they have given me for the rest of my life.

Here's my list (so far!):

1. Laugh a LOT! Laugh from the gut. Bellow. Purge. Affirm. Guffaw. NEVER take life or yourself too seriously.
2. Make your own fun regularly. You have the power to give your life meaning. Plan a creative party. Sew something new. Try a new recipe. Create your own games.
3. Sing! Don't worry about your voice.
4. Spend some time just with women. Affirm the sacred bond between them.
5. Value memories over things. Love and friendship are more important than all the money in the world.
6. Savor sunsets.
7. Nap daily.
8. Celebrate birthdays!
9. Create your own rituals. Rituals keep us connected to our lives, the earth, and one another.
10. Honor children.

Make your own list. What have you learned from the powerful women in your life?

ACTIVITY

Words of Encouragement

One of my friends is an artist whose ideas usually inspire me to jump out of my chair and create. One of his techniques is putting speech bubbles on photos of famous people or of people he admires. The bubbles are filled with good tidings and words of encouragement. One day I ran home to try this technique, and it works! It's one of my favorite things to do and it always makes me giggle. Plus, it's always nice to hear positive feedback from the people whom you most admire. Fill your wall!

Here's what you do:
1. Find a photo of a person whom you really admire. It could be your parents, Maya Angelou, Mother Teresa, the Buddha, the Dalai Lama, Albert Einstein, even yourself, if you like.
2. Write an affirmation or words of encouragement in the bubble. Make it something you want to read every day.
3. Cut out the bubble and glue or tape it to the photo. Hang it in a prominent place. Feel good.

Become Your Own **SUPERHERO** *template*

Directions:

1. Think of qualities you would like to develop. Look at the *Superhero* comic for ideas.

2. Cut out the template, and start to create your *Superhero* self. Draw in your face, your hair, etc., or use photos of yourself.

3. Create your own outfits & accessories. Make them unique to **YOU!**

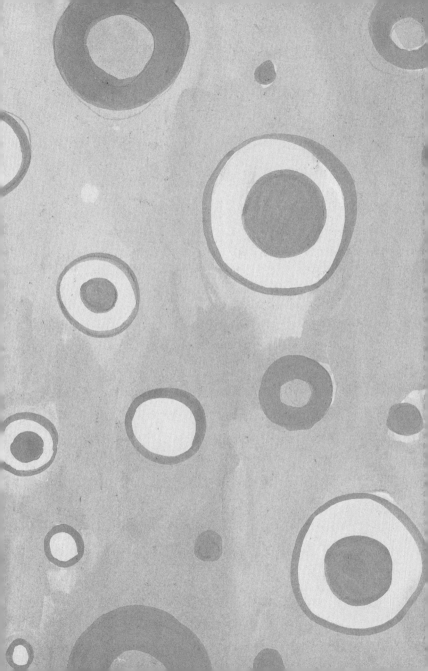

Directions for Making a Magic Book

Use 1 sheet of 8½ × 11

(out of one sheet of paper!)

It's easy!

1. Fold the sheet in half lengthwise. Open it flat again.

2. Fold it in half the other direction. Open it flat again.

3. Fold the bottom up to meet the middle. Open it flat again.

middle

4. Fold the top down to meet the middle. Open it flat again.

middle

5. Fold in half vertically again and cut a slit.

from here to here

6. Holding each end push them together so you can see through the slit. (It should make a diamond shape.)

7. Push the ends in further until it looks like a plus sign.

← A plus sign

8. Flatten it so you have two pages on each side.

9. Fold the whole thing in half. You now have your very own book!

Letting Go

Solitude

I learned . . . that inspiration does not come like a bolt, nor is it kinetic, energetic striving, but it comes into us slowly and quietly and all the time, though we must regularly and every day give it a little chance to start flowing, prime it with a little solitude and idleness.
—Brenda Ueland

We need to fight the urge to compulsively plan our days, to hurry back to work, to worry about people trying to reach us, to fret about a job that is due, to think about what we should be doing. The creative mind does not work well under this pressure.

I've learned that slowly walking without purpose or designation is the best form of therapy. When I slow down, I notice the color of the snow, the smell of the air, the feel of the wind, and the hundreds of animal tracks just off the trail—and new ideas start to flow in. By letting go of all the clutter in your mind, you allow the good, intuitive stuff to surface. You make room for what your soul is seeking, and you get in touch with what you really want. It's not as easy as it sounds, but it is the way to the present moment.

CELEBRATE SOLITUDE!!!
It seems that what the body does, the mind soon follows. When we're in solitude, ideas flow almost effortlessly. Our muse is but a deep breath and a long slow walk away. Enjoy the process of meeting up with it again.

Rituals to Propel You to Your Greatest Potential

Rituals are deliberate actions used to shift our perceptions or to transform an experience. They are most helpful during a time of transition (new school), during a time of intense change (a marriage or a loss), or when we need to conjure up feelings of strength (before a big job interview). In developing your own rituals, you can start by creating a small event that represents the bigger events in your life.

Use these rituals when you need to smooth transitions, embrace fears, or manifest gratitude.

New Life Seeds
Plant seeds indoors or outdoors to acknowledge big change. Let their growth represent your own forward movement.

Confidence Song
Choose an empowering anthem to give you strength. I've used "The Confidence Song" from *The Sound of Music* for years. It has never failed to give me a boost.

Smudging

Smudging is a Native American technique in which certain herbs are burned to create a cleansing smoke bath. The smoke is used to purify people, creative spaces, and objects. Smudging is helpful when you want to change the energy in a space and start fresh, when you are feeling unmotivated, during your meditation practice, or as a form of prayer. I find it particularly useful after finishing a difficult job. You can purchase a smudge stick at a health food or New Age store, or you can make your own. (See page 68 for instructions).

Decorate "Just Because"

Hang lights or stars from the ceiling for a magical effect. This ritual helps to encourage daily motivation or new life in a work space.

Manifest Abundance

Make a Wish Jar (see page 95) to manifest abundance.

How to make a Smudge Stick

You will need:
- Branches of herbs (rosemary, sage, lavender, artemesia, pine, or juniper)
- Newspaper
- Rubber bands
- Colored string
- Scissors or garden shears

1. Gather a bunch of branches together (1 inch diameter). Trim the branches to make them all the same size. (large = 6 in. long or small = 3 in. long)

2. Lay the bundle at the edge of one sheet of newspaper and roll the bundle tightly. Place rubber bands around it to keep it together.

roll

3. Put it in a warm place to dry.

4. After about 2 weeks, remove the paper. Wrap the sticks with string.

To Use: Carefully light one end of the stick with a match. Wait a moment and blow out the flame. Blow on the end to encourage smoke. Hold over a plate and carry through your home or to areas that need purifying!

ACTIVITY

Write a Letter to Yourself in the Future

TIME CAPSULE

1. Write a letter to read five, ten, or twenty years from today.
2. Place the letter in a strongbox along with an object of significance.
3. Bury it in a safe place. (If you prefer, hide it in your attic or a special place where no one will find it.)
4. When the time feels right, dig it up and marvel at who you've become.

Take a Mini-Vacation

Imagination is the voice of the daring.
                                        —Henry Miller

Today I packed a bag with my journal, a sweater, and a bottle of water, and I set off for my mini-vacation spot, a small lake where I go to get away from it all. It's quiet, secluded, calming, magical, stunningly beautiful, and it's only a five-minute walk from my house.

I sat by the water surrounded by tall pine trees and geese, and I pretended that I'd traveled for days to reach this spot. I left behind the deadlines, structure, and routine of my life. I stretched out on the shore with my book and wrote whatever came into my head. I occasionally paused, my pen hovering over the page, to listen to the frogs singing, the birds diving, and the fish jumping.

I'm amazed at how freeing it is to take myself on a mini-vacation. Everything is fresh and new through the eyes of a traveler. I exist in the present moment and I am drawn to playful, childlike pursuits like skipping rocks, napping outdoors, watching the clouds, and climbing trees.

I've collected a pile of stones by the lake. It's an

ancient method of marking my territory and letting others know the spot is sacred. On every visit I add a few more stones to the pile, noticing from week to week if it has changed with the weather, or by the hand of an unknown visitor.

Take Your Own Mini-Vacation
Find somewhere close to your home or office. It could be a park, a greenhouse, a cemetery, or a waterfront. Make it your OWN special place. Make a decision to look at things as if seeing them for the first time. A small cafe in any city could easily become the south of France. A bike ride on a country lane could become a jaunt through the German countryside. A sunny garden could become a Tuscan adventure. Let your imagination wander . . . Bon voyage!

How to have a (free) Mini-Vacation

without leaving home

You can easily create the feeling of a "real" vacation wherever you are. It requires only a small shift in perception and a few helpful tools. Packing a bag gives the feeling of going away and creates a portable comfort zone. Here are some things to include:

a special beverage (keep hydrated)

Your best walking hat.

sunglasses

a favorite sweater (so you can adapt to weather changes)

Snacks to keep your energy up!

Inspiring literature (May Sarton & Sark are 2 of my faves!)

HOUSE BY THE SEA / Creative Companion

Journal / Crayons

*most important for when sudden inspiration hits, or just to doodle.

Some change. (For coffee on a patio?)

Dear...

Postcards to send to friends!

lip balm

swim suit

Directions:

City: Wander aimlessly (be a tourist)! Let serendipity take over!

Country: Find a secluded spot, preferably by water. Set up camp. Toss stones.

LIVING WITH LESS AND ENJOYING IT MORE

I was introduced to wabi-sabi while taking a course in Eastern philosophy, but it was some time later before I really grasped its "less is more" concept. Wabi-sabi is a Japanese concept that speaks to the art of imperfection, and/or the willingness to accept things as they are. Wabi-sabi is about process, not product. It is about decay and aging, not growth. Wabi-sabi requires that we slow down to take notice of hidden things, imperfections, and the passing of time. If you like control, it takes courage and trust to practice wabi-sabi.

One day my partner and I had decided to spend a few hours together sketching outdoors, and to make a game of choosing the subject matter. When it was his turn, he chose a thin stick. My immediate reaction was, "We're surrounded by luscious nature, and you choose a dead stick?" Reluctantly, I took out my pen and started to draw.

At first, all I could see was the outline of the stick. Straight lines. A hook at the top. After five minutes, I started to see the play of light and shadow. In fifteen minutes, I noticed tiny marks, indents, and shading. After a half-hour, this simple stick had become something living, moving, and expanding. It was transformed into an intricate object right in front of me. *This* was wabi-sabi.

To practice wabi-sabi means to accept nature's process, including impermanence and the absence of life. You can start by taking notice of the details in your everyday life. A spiderweb full of dead bugs in the window frame. An old chair with chipped paint. A yellowed newspaper. These things could be dismissed as ugly and without value, but wabi-sabi teaches us that we are in a constant state of change and we must value that which is in the moment.

🦋 Transformative Play
in the garden

encourage friends to add ribbons

Play with dirt! Plant seeds for fun or make a Zen garden with just sand and rocks.

Hang Prayer Ribbons
① Write prayers or wishes on colorful pieces of string.
② Tie them to a string suspended over the garden.

Each step is the place to learn.

Go with nature & she's easy and delicious! E.C.

Paint wildly colored banners with your favorite quotes.

Paint rocks because it's fun. Lay them all around the garden. (use them as markers for flowers.) **Create an herb garden based on smell.**

Line a pathway with candles for an evening of ambience. (write with chalk on the path.)

venture ad new a to way my on I'm

Make an Herb bed.
1. Fill a large box with soil.
2. Plant herbs (Chamomile or Thyme work well for this.)
3. Encourage everyone to lie in it.

please lie down

(the smell is sleep inducing and you won't harm the herbs.)

Living out LOUD Calendar

1. Fill in the dates for the next month with a pencil.
2. Use the stickers to schedule in special things to do for yourself.

SUN	MON	TUES	WED	THURS	FRI	SAT

Mini-Vacation

Sense Shopping

Special Dinner

Spa Day

Research/Reading

Dare to Dream *dream*

Buy Flowers

Nap

P.J. Party

Do Nothing Day

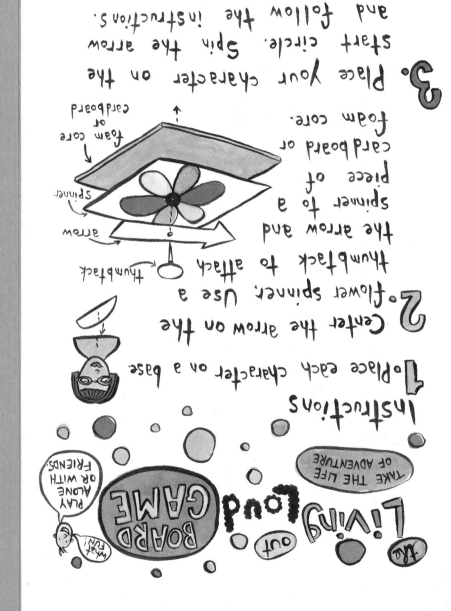

Living Loud out BOARD GAME

TAKE THE LIFE OF ADVENTURE

PLAY ALONE OR WITH FRIENDS!

what fun!

Instructions

1. Place each character on a base.

2. Center the arrow on the flower spinner. Use a thumbtack to attach the arrow and spinner to a piece of cardboard or foam core.

3. Place your character on the start circle. Spin the arrow and follow the instructions.

cardboard

foam core or cardboard

spinner

arrow

thumbtack

Dreaming Work

How to Make a Living Doing What You Love

1. Ask Yourself What You Want

Be specific. Figuring out exactly what you want will help you FOCUS on where you need to go. Write it down. What are your deepest dreams? Take them seriously and they will lead to what you really want.

Create INTENT in your life to manifest your dreams in the physical world. Defining an Unlimited Life Plan (one that expresses all your wildest dreams) is one of the most valuable things you can do. Start with a personal philosophy and mission statement. Make a list with two columns. Label the first "Objectives," for example, "create an identity within my industry." Label the second "Actions," such as "write an article for a magazine." When you truly commit to your goal, the money will appear!

2. Believe That You Can

If you follow one piece of advice on your path, let it be this: Replace "What if I'm not cut out for this?" with an affirmative "YES I CAN!" Most successful people are ingrained with this quality, but anyone can learn. Get "can't" out of your vocabulary. Stay away from people who say, "You can't make a living at it." (There will be many.) Repeat this mantra with feeling: "There are people out there in need of my services!"

3. Research

Find people who are already making a living doing what you want to do. Read about them. Make them into a model for your career and your life. Connect with them—most successful people are happy to talk to those starting down the same path. Read any book you can about triumph over adversity; it will help you through those days when you question your choices. Create a support network of people in your field. Try to meet with them regularly; it will help you feel normal.

4. Pretend You Already Are Who You Want to Be

And you will become it! No one starts off in any field feeling confident and powerful. It takes time to build and grow. Sometimes it feels like you're not moving at all. There will be other times when you feel like you're faking it. ("What if someone figures me out?") It's O.K. No one knows but you.

5. Ignore . . .

Those who tell you it can't be done.
Those who have tried and given up.
Those who think you're nuts to throw away a regular income and try something new.

Most people yearn to do what they love for a living, but many believe they can't afford the risks or handle the responsibilities. Scared people will impose their own fears on you. Let them know how happy your work makes you. Let go of friends who don't understand what you're trying to do and surround yourself with people who support your new choices.

6. Prioritize

Make your work a priority. Your work and your life are not separate entities. You need to have energy to build a career. We have been taught that we must work full time to maintain a certain lifestyle. Let go of this belief and consider alternatives. Subsidize your income with part-time or contract work. Scale down your living expenses. (Do you really need two bedrooms? Can you relocate?) ASK FOR HELP when you need it!!! There is someone out there right now who can help you. Take a look at the books in the Business section.

7. Feel the Fear

I've talked to many people who have worked for years doing what they love and THEY STILL HAVE FEAR! I was amazed to find that success sometimes brings more fear—the fear of living up to the expectations and reputation of previous successes. If the fear is always there, you might as well learn to manage it instead of trying to get rid of it.

8. Reinvent Yourself

You are not defined by your current situation. You can start fresh at any given time. After failures (I prefer to call them lessons), get back on your feet and start again. Writers will be rejected. Illustrators will send out work they hate. Freelancers will have dry periods. Designers will have quotes rejected. There is always an ebb and flow to success, money, fame, and creative energy. DUST YOURSELF OFF.

9. BEGIN NOW!!!

The circumstances will never be perfect. You will never have enough money saved. Your portfolio will never be ready. You may never have the perfect space, studio, or equipment. These are self-limiting beliefs created by our inner critic. You will not have the time if you don't make it NOW.

Don't make a big production out of it. Use what you've got! Ernest Hemingway wrote on napkins. Keith Haring painted subway stations. Charles and Ray Eames designed and made chairs in a tiny bedroom. You have everything in your possession right now to start moving toward your goals. When you take a small step in the direction of your dream, the universe often takes several more for you.

10. Let Go

Don't worry about your talent or capability. It is not yours to judge, and it will grow and change over time. Do not ask, "Why am I doing this? Is this right?" Freaking out about what you *should* be doing does not move you forward. ENJOY THE PROCESS. Starting can be the most overwhelming part, but it is also exciting and full of possibilities. Change can be intimidating, unfamiliar, terrifying, and downright uncomfortable. Your life is too rich, and you are too powerful, to have anything less than what you truly deserve. You have a responsibility to do what you love every day, to become your most authentic, powerful self, to share your passion with the rest of the world, and to live up to the spirit that is in you.

The universe is waiting . . .

the WISH jar...

I WISH...

...is a powerful receptacle for all the dreams and wishes in your **life**, especially those that you think are impossible! There is an unseen power that starts to work when you put your innermost desires on paper. See for yourself, but be prepared... you **will** get what you ask for.

1. Find an old mason jar. (the kind with a screwtop lid)

2. Cut a hole in the lid. (I used a screwdriver with a hammer to punch it)

glass

MASON

3. Think of things that might make your life _more_ fulfilled, luscious, or spectacular. They can be big things | I want a house in the country. | or small things. | I want purple galoshes. | Write down as many as you can think of.

4. Put them in the jar. Watch them come **True!**

ACTIVITY

Lifestyle for Sale

This is a really fun exercise! It reminds me of when I was little and used to create miniature dream homes out of clay.

In recent years, lifestyle stores have become the rage, selling products related to all aspects of living: eating, decorating, reading, bathing, sleeping, and dressing.

My lifestyle store would be in an old funky house. The walls would be light and calming, but the contents of the store would radiate with color. The items for sale would include colorful Japanese paper, many flavors of tea, teapots, fresh flowers, soothing fragrances, and definitely pajamas. There would be beautiful journals and paintbrushes, and bottles of colored ink. Old books could be found on little bookshelves. Quotes would be posted everywhere. I would display mysterious toys and objects from foreign lands. My store would evolve and change, and I would add to my store when more ideas flooded in.

If you were to open your own lifestyle store, what would you sell?

Make a list of what it would contain. Draw pictures of what it would look like. What items best represent you and your many layers? Are they eclectic? Chaotic? Minimal? Calming? What kind of space would be appropriate for you? Would it be a large loft, or a room full of nooks and crannies in an old Victorian house? What colors would you use? Come up with a name for your store—maybe it's a character from your favorite book, or something that reflects the store's contents.

Organizing your creative space 🍕

🧦 ...for those who live in PILES

Lessons from a professional Mess-maker

Highly creative people are often quite disorganized. Maybe it has to do with the right side of the brain not caring about time & space. Here are a few tricks to help with this. (You may never be fully cured.)

1. Make it FUN!
Use brightly colored boxes or bins. Use paint or paper.

PAPER   GLUE

2. Make it easy.
I use open bins so I can dump stuff easily

Pastels   Craft   PAINT

Try this:
Make a special motivation area with fresh flowers & candles

3. LABEL everything.
So you always put it back

Designation is the key— remember that saying your mother taught you, "There's a place for everything." Spend five minutes a day putting things away.

A great way to hang your work is on a clothesline against the wall. Cheap, yet très chic!

LEARNING TO TRUST YOURSELF

*Watch yourself. Every minute we change. It is a
great opportunity. At any point, we can step out
of our frozen selves and our ideas and begin fresh.*
    —Natalie Goldberg

Some years back, I had to face the decision to end
a significant professional relationship. I asked the
universe for help but didn't listen to its answers.
Instead, I went to friends, fellow illustrators, and
anyone who would listen. I called other people to
reaffirm my beliefs. I looked for the quick fix—no
hard work, no inner searching—just make it easy.
I trusted the opinions of others over my own.

It's really tough to trust yourself.

Do you know, deep down, what's right for you but still
don't trust? Are you like me, picturing things in your
head that may not be real? (I have a tendency to play
a movie in my head of the future, based purely on my
own assumptions; these assumptions are sometimes
based on my fears and doubts and have little to do
with reality.) Do you fear a big decision will impact
others negatively or upset somebody? Do you attempt
to control a situation before it happens? Do you fear
making the wrong decision? Are you pressured by

perfection? Do you fear the unknown? Success?
Conflict? Is it tempting to stay in a familiar place
because it is safe, even though you know it is not the
best for you? How do you know what is right for you?

Listen to your body. Those gut feelings, spine tingles,
and goose bumps are messages that something is
up. Try asking, "How does my body feel right now?"
instead of asking, "How do I feel about this?" How
do you ACT on what you are feeling?

Trusting yourself requires . . .
1. **Practice.** Take baby steps. Say no when a friend
   asks you to do something you don't really want
   to do. It will get easier each time.
2. **Discipline.** Be strong in your resolve to put
   yourself first.
3. **Commitment.** Make a commitment not to take
   the safe route.
4. **Surrender.** Let things happen naturally and try
   not to anticipate the situation. You may be surprised
   at the outcome. The universe will send signs to let
   you know you are doing the right thing. Let go of
   all assumptions.

Here's my mantra, which you may borrow:
*I am grateful for the ability to learn from this situation.
I will do my best to help myself move forward and into
my greatest, most powerful potential!*

ACTIVITY

Let's Pretend

Pretend for one day, or even an hour, that you already are who you want to be. Act as if you are living the life that you've always imagined. Where do you create your work? How do you spend your time? What are you wearing? How does your work space reflect your personality?

Use what you have—don't worry if it's just a spot in your basement. Think big. You might need a phone to call your agent, or a day planner to schedule all your public appearances. Maybe you're an artist. Jackson Pollock liked to paint on the floor of his studio. Roll out newsprint and doodle. Maybe you're a movie star. What kind of special treatment do you require? Get into character.

Personal Myths

EMBRACING THE DARK

Many of us have parts of our personalities that we would rather not deal with. These parts often are labeled during our childhood and teenage years, and the labels stick. They become myths about our personalities.

I had a teacher in art school who taught me a good lesson about labels. He asked me, "How tall are you?" I was kind of surprised by the question and replied, "Five feet, seven and three-quarters inches." He looked intrigued and asked, "How tall do you think I am?" I stood back and made a quick assessment. He had always struck me as a short person, so I guessed, "Five feet, three inches." He laughed, and then we stood back to back. I was stunned to see we were the same height!

He proceeded to tell me that he was always the shortest kid in school and that he had carried this perception through his life. It was his personal myth—a label that was pinned on him—but it was completely untrue. Because of his belief about himself, as he aged he continued to project his image of shortness to the world.

For years I had carried myths about myself that were incredibly dysfunctional. I pictured them as little pieces of paper pinned to my clothes. One of the biggest ones was "never finishes anything." I felt broken. I sabotaged my early attempts at becoming a highly functional artist and person by holding onto these myths. But then I discovered that my dark side was extremely valuable to my creative endeavors. Things I had been taught were negative were actually my greatest strengths. The key was to shift my perception, and to use the negatives in my life and my work. For example, while the label "naïve" once hindered me, I now believe it is one of my greatest gifts. I now see myself as trusting and open to good karma. I was called a procrastinator, a label that bothered me. Now I see this as a good thing and never limit my playtime, because I never know when it will lead to my next big idea. I've been called "messy"; I choose to see this as "intensely creative" and it's made a world of difference.

We all have the power to reinvent our personal myths by transforming our perception.

Here's a formula for reinvention:
Embrace the so-called bad stuff in a new way. Use your dark side to your advantage. Let it become part of your new myth. Don't fix it—feature it. Let it play a starring role in your creative life.

ACTIVITY

Getting it Out

Take notice of the language you use in your daily life.
Do you use words like "good" and "bad"? "Like" and
"dislike"? "Love" and "hate"? These are words we use
to judge others and ourselves. Consider letting go of
these words. Try to get beyond the need to critique.
You have the choice to view life differently. When
judgment comes up, replace it with the mantra: "I
allow my expressions to come out clearly and directly.
It is my job to keep the channel open. It is fine as it
is. Let it be."

make a Magic Pocket Shrine

final product

art

Originating in Mexico, the pocket shrine is both a creative and a *symbolic* act used to enhance a part of your life. Think about which part you would like to bring new life to. Possible topics might be:

creativity Prosperity healing love STRENGTH
dreams abundance courage peace

e.g.: icons, saints, money, people

time to make 1 hour

glue   glue

glue   glue

Cut along solid lines

Collect:
- Imagery of what you are trying to create.
- Words, quotes, poems, buttons, sequins, beads, feathers, fabric, newspaper, cards, seeds, tiny candles, toys, Japanese paper.

How to Assemble:

the doors open & close

1. Cut out box.
2. Fold along dotted lines.
3. Apply glue to tabs. Glue into box shape!
4. Collage to reinforce the box. Coat it with glue.

The Hard Part

I recently formed a club with an inspiring group of women, to share ideas, drink wine, and talk about books. One night it was suggested that we present our own writing to the group. I was surprised when several women reacted with "My writing is horrible" and "That would be devastating."

Why do we believe that we have nothing valuable to say? Why do we believe that our thoughts and ideas are not important enough to put on paper?

The fear of being compared to others and the expectation of perfection gets in the way of writing and other creative activities. When you compare yourself to others, you feel terrible and drained, but when you allow your work to be what it is without judgment, you become empowered. Practice the Buddhist principle of non-judgment. Think: "I can do it, too!"

Each human being has a unique path. When you follow in someone else's footsteps (or yearn for another's success), you are not being honest or authentic. It's scary to be in unknown territory, but it is the only way to your truly powerful destination. Acknowledge the uniqueness of your life. Let this be your deep well of creative ideas and *get it out*.

Permission Cards

LIVING ON PURPOSE DAILY

Permission Cards take the frenzy out of your hectic existence and give you permission to do what you REALLY want.

Directions
1. Tear out the cards.
2. Place the cards in a bowl.
3. Close your eyes and pick one.
   (The one that you need will stick to your fingers.)
4. Say out loud, "I now have permission to _____."

meditate

vent

CHANGE

INSPIRE

SIMPLIFY

trust

smile

grow

dance

empower

let go

accept

contribute

choose

love

WISH

dream

create

Begin

TRY

forgive

nap

LAUGH

investigate

express

transform

bloom

invent

receive

EMBRACE

recharge

PLAY

Heal

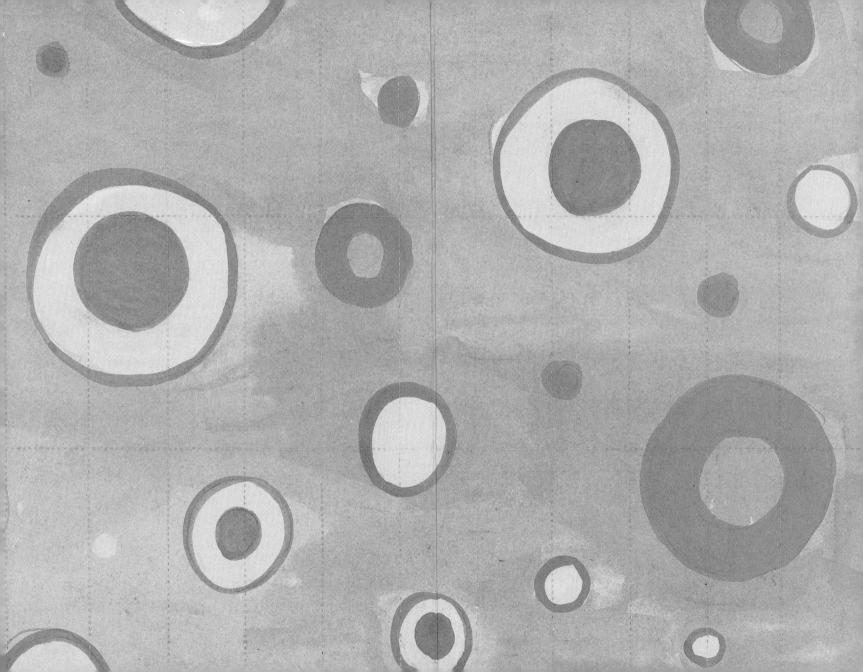

Living Out Loud
Personal Manifesto

I, _____, hereby choose to make
the following beliefs a part of
my daily life...

... make play a priority.
... dream expansively.
... live out LOUD.
... create abundance.
... treat myself like a queen.
...reinvent myself when necessary.
... give back to the world.
...encourage gratitude.
...challenge my greatest fears.
...recognize my unique talents & gifts.
... share these gifts with the world.
...surround myself with beauty.
... release all judgment of
my creative expression.

Bibliography

Courage, Triumph over Adversity and Fear
Angelou, Maya. *I Know Why the Caged Bird Sings.*
New York: Random House, 1970.

———. *Wouldn't Take Nothing for My Journey Now.*
New York: Random House, 1993.

Campbell, Joseph. *The Hero with a Thousand Faces.*
Princeton: Bollingen Series, Princeton University
Press, 1949.

Coelho, Paulo. *The Alchemist: A Fable about Following
Your Dream.* Translated by Alan R. Clarke. San
Francisco: HarperSanFrancisco, 1993.

Colette. *Earthly Paradise: An Autobiography of Colette
Drawn from Her Lifetime Writings.* Edited by Robert
Phelps. New York: Farrar, Straus & Giroux, 1975.

Frank, Anne. *Anne Frank: The Diary of a Young
Girl—The Definitive Edition.* Edited by Otto H. Frank
and Mirjam Pressler. New York: Doubleday, 1995.

Frankl, Viktor E. *Man's Search for Meaning.* New
York: Simon & Schuster, 1963.

Hanh, Thich Nhat. *Peace in Every Step: The Path of Mindfulness in Everyday Life.* New York: Bantam, 1992.

Hoff, Benjamin, ed. *The Singing Creek Where the Willows Grow: The Mystical Nature Diary of Opal Whiteley.* New York: Penguin, 1995.

———. *The Tao of Pooh.* New York: E.P. Dutton, 1982.

Lindbergh, Anne Morrow. *Gift from the Sea.* New York: Pantheon, 1955.

Myss, Caroline. *Anatomy of the Spirit: The Seven Stages of Power and Healing.* New York: Random House, 1997.

Nin, Anaïs. *The Diary of Anaïs Nin, Volume I, 1931–1934.* Edited with an introduction by Gunther Stuhlmann. San Diego: Harcourt, 1975.

Northrup, Christiane. W*omen's Bodies, Women's Wisdom: Creating Physical and Emotional Health and Healing.* New York: Bantam, 1998.

Osbon, Diane K., ed. *A Joseph Campbell Companion: Reflections on the Art of Living.* New York: HarperCollins, 1992.

Pilgrim, Peace. *Peace Pilgrim: Her Life and Work in Her Own Words.* Sante Fe: Ocean Tree Books, 1991.

SARK. *Inspiration Sandwich: Stories to Inspire Our Creative Freedom.* Berkeley: Celestial Arts, 1992.

Sarton, May. *Journal of a Solitude.* New York: Norton, 1973.

———. *Plant Dreaming Deep.* New York: Norton, 1968.

Zukav, Gary. *The Seat of the Soul.* New York: Simon & Schuster, 1989.

Creativity
Bender, Sue. *Everyday Sacred: A Woman's Journey Home.* San Francisco: HarperSanFrancisco, 1995.

Breathnach, Sarah Ban. *Simple Abundance: A Daybook of Comfort and Joy.* New York: Warner, 1995.

Cameron, Julia. *The Artist's Way: A Spiritual Path to Higher Creativity.* New York: Tarcher/Putnam, 1992.

———. *The Vein of Gold: A Journey to Your Creative Heart.* New York: Tarcher/Putnam, 1996.

Cerwinske, Laura. *Writing as a Healing Art: The Transforming Power of Self-Expression.* New York: Perigee, 1999.

Goldberg, Natalie. *Long Quiet Highway: Waking Up in America.* New York: Bantam, 1993.

―――. *Wild Mind: Living the Writer's Life.* New York: Bantam, 1990.

―――. *Writing Down the Bones: Freeing the Writer Within.* Reprint, with a foreword by Judith Guest. Boston: Shambhala Publications, 1996.

Kent, Corita, and Jan Steward. *Learning by Heart: Teachings to Free the Creative Spirit.* New York: Bantam, 1992.

Koren, Leonard. *Wabi-Sabi: For Artists, Designers, Poets, and Philosophers.* Berkeley: Stone Bridge Press, 1994.

Miller, Henry. *Stand Still Like the Hummingbird.* New York: Norton, 1962.

―――. *The Wisdom of the Heart.* New York: New Directions, 1941.

SARK. *A Creative Companion: How to Free Your Creative Spirit.* Berkeley: Celestial Arts, 1991.

Ueland, Brenda. *If You Want to Write: A Book about Art, Independence, and Spirit.* 1938. Reprint, Saint Paul, Minn.: Graywolf Press, 1987.

Wood, Beatrice. *I Shock Myself: The Autobiography of Beatrice Wood.* Reprint, edited by Lindsay Smith. Ojai, Calif.: Dillingham Press, 1985.

Authors to Research

Dillard, Annie. *Pilgrim at Tinker Creek.* New York: Harper Perennial, 1998.

Emerson, Ralph Waldo. *The Essential Writings of Ralph Waldo Emerson.* Princeton: Princeton Review, 2000.

Haring, Keith. *Keith Haring Journals.* New York: Penguin USA, 1997.

Jesus, Carolina Maria. *I'm Going to Have a Little House: The Second Diary of Carolina Maria Jesus.* Translated by Melvin S. Arrington, Jr., and Robert M. Levine. Lincoln: University of Nebraska Press, 1997.

Lamott, Anne. *Traveling Mercies: Some Thoughts on Faith.* New York: Anchor Books, 1999.

Thoreau, Henry David. *Walden.* 1854. Reprint with an introduction and annotations by Bill McKibben. Boston: Beacon Press, 1998.

Truitt, Anne. *Daybook: The Journal of an Artist.* New York: Viking Press, 1982.

Visual Journals

Eldon, Dan. *The Journey Is the Destination: The Journals of Dan Eldon.* San Francisco: Chronicle Books, 1997.

Fanelli, Sara. *Dear Diary.* Cambridge, Mass.: Candlewick Press, 2000.

Hall, Peter, ed. *Tibor Kalman: Perverse Optimist.* Princeton: Princeton Architectural Press, 1998.

Harrison, Sabrina Ward. *Spilling Open: The Art of Becoming Yourself.* New York: Villard, 2000.

Jernigan, Candy. *Evidence: The Art of Candy Jernigan.* San Francisco: Chronicle Books, 1999.

Kahlo, Frida, Carlos Fuentes, and Sarah M. Lowe. *The Diary of Frida Kahlo: An Intimate Self-Portrait.* New York: Abradale, 2000.

Knowles, Alison. *Footnotes: Collage Journal Thirty Years.* New York: Granary Books, 2000.

Laurel, Alicia Bay. *Living on the Earth.* New York: Random House, 1972.

Midda, Sara. *Sara Midda's South of France: A Sketch Book.* New York: Workman, 1990.

Nelson, Beth. *Postcards from the Basque Country: A Journey of Enchantment and Imagination.* New York: Stewart, Tabori & Chang, 1999.

Price, Dan. *Moonlight Chronicles: A Wandering Artist's Journal.* Berkeley: Ten Speed Press, 2000.

Business and Money

Elgin, Duane. *Voluntary Simplicity: Toward a Way of Life That Is Outwardly Simple, Inwardly Rich.* Revised ed. New York: Quill, 1993.

Foote, Cameron S. *The Business Side of Creativity: The Complete Guide for Running a Graphic Design or Communications Business.* New York: Norton, 1996.

Franks, Lynne. *The Seed Handbook: The Feminine Way to Create Business.* New York: Tarcher/Putnam, 2000.

Glickman, Marshall. *The Mindful Money Guide: Creating Harmony between Your Values and Your Finances.* New York: Ballantine, 1999.

Orman, Suze. *The Nine Steps to Financial Freedom: Practical and Spiritual Steps So You Can Stop Worrying.* New York: Crown, 1997.

Phillips, Michael, and Salli Rasberry. *Honest Business: A Superior Strategy for Starting and Managing Your Own Business.* Boston: Shambhala Publications, 1996.

———. *Marketing without Advertising.* 3rd ed. Berkeley: Nolo Press, 2001

———. *The Seven Laws of Money.* San Francisco: Clear Glass Publishing, 2002.

Pierce, Linda Breen, and Vicki Robin. *Choosing Simplicity: Real People Finding Peace and Fulfillment in a Complex World.* Carmel, Calif.: Gallagher Press, 2000.

Roman, Sanaya, and Duane Packer. *Creating Money: Keys to Abundance.* Tiburon, Calif.: H. J. Kramer, 1988.

Whitmyer, Claude, and Salli Rasberry. *Running a One-Person Business.* 2nd ed. Berkeley: Ten Speed Press, 1994.

Yudkin, Marcia. *Six Steps to Free Publicity: And Dozens of Other Ways to Win Free Media Attention for You or Your Business.* New York: Plume, 1994.

Acknowledgments

I would like to thank all who were my teachers (and still are). You are always with me. Linda Montgomery, Dr. Bryant Griffith, Shirley Yanover, Ross Mendes, Hanna Legrow, Marion and Doug Smith, Jennifer Smith, Judy Stittle, Sandy Bain, Corita Kent, Charles and Ray Eames, Henry Miller, May Sarton, Anaïs Nin, SARK, Beatrice Wood, Emily Carr, Lynda Barry, Maya Angelou, Martha Graham, Arno Verhoeven, and my new family in Flesherton.

Biography

Keri Smith is an award-winning illustrator and author who has dedicated her life to creative living and the promotion of "play." She lives in a small cottage in the country and spends her time painting, dancing, reading, singing, giving lectures, writing in her journal, and creating playful products and books. She has written and illustrated two children's projects published by Chronicle Books: *Story in a Box: Cinderella* and *Story in a Box: The Princess and the Pea*. For more information, please visit www.kerismith.com.

from *Living Out Loud*
published by Chronicle Books © 2003 Keri Smith

Everybody is original, if they tell the truth, if they speak from their true self. But it must be from their true self and not from the self they think they should be. So remember these two things: you are talented and you are ORIGINAL.

Brenda Ueland

Know that there is often hidden in us a dormant POET, always young and ALIVE.

- de Musset

from *Living Out Loud*
published by Chronicle Books © 2003 Keri Smith

Inspiration is intention obeyed.

—emily carr

Each day, and the living of it, has to be a conscious creation in which discipline and order are relieved with some play and pure foolishness.

May Sarton

Go confidently in the
direction of your dreams
Live the life you've imagined
As you simplify your life
The laws of the universe
will be simpler.

— Thoreau

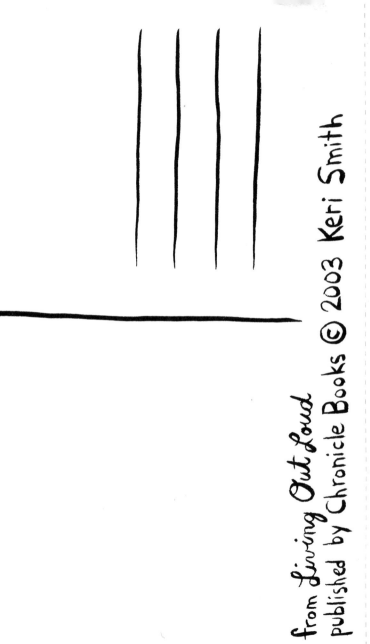